FIRST THOUSAND WORDS

IN ENGLISH

Heather Amery

Illustrated by Stephen Cartwright

Revised edition by Mairi Mackinnon
Picture editing by Mike Olley

There is a little yellow duck to look for on every
double page with pictures. Can you find it?

Stephen Cartwright's little yellow duck made his first-ever appearance in *The First Thousand Words* over thirty years ago. Duck has since featured in over 125 titles, in more than 70 languages, and has delighted millions of readers, both young and old, around the world.

This revised edition first published in 2013 by Usborne Publishing Ltd, 83-85 Saffron Hill, London EC1N 8RT. www.usborne.com
Based on a previous title first published in 1979. Copyright © 2013, 1995, 1979 Usborne Publishing Ltd.

First published in America in 2013.

About this book

This picture word book has been designed to appeal to children at different ages, and can be used in various ways. This edition has been brought up to date to include words and objects which are common in everyday language and familiar in everyday life.

paints

A wordbuilder for young children
For very young children, it is a bright and stimulating way of learning new words. The large pictures provide lots of opportunities for spotting and matching with the smaller pictures around the edges, and for discussing the lively scenes.

bottles

A reading and spelling guide for older children
For older children, the book can be used in the early stages of learning to read, and as a beginner's guide to spelling.

A vocabulary builder for English language learners
For children learning English as a second or additional language, it is a powerful and effective way of learning to read, say and spell new words.

goldfish

Hear the words online
You can listen to all the words in the book on the Usborne website. Just go to **www.usborne.com/quicklinks** and enter the keywords **1000 English**. There you can also find links to other useful websites about the English language, Britain and the USA.

helicopter

Using the wordlist
At the back of the book there is a list of all the words in alphabetical order. It can be used to encourage children to look up words and find the right page and picture. This is an important skill which will prepare children to use simple information books and dictionaries.

jigsaw puzzle

Remember, this is a book of a thousand words. It will take time to learn them all. This is a book to come back to again and again.

chocolate

At home

bathtub

soap

faucet

toilet paper

toothbrush

water

toilet

sponge

sink

shower

towel

bed

bathroom

living room

toothpaste

radio

cushion

DVD

carpet

sofa

4

 chair

 comforter

 comb

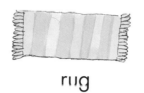 sheet

 rug

 closet

bedroom

 television

 chest of drawers

 mirror

 brush

hall

lamp

 pictures

 coat rack

 telephone

 radiator

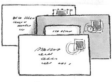 fruit

newspaper

 table

 letters

 stairs

5

The kitchen

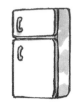
refrigerator

glasses

clock

stool

teaspoons

switch

laundry detergent

key

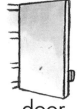
door

sink

vacuum cleaner

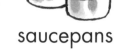

saucepans

forks

apron

ironing board

trash

6

kettle

knives

mop

dust cloth

tiles

broom

washing
machine

dustpan

drawer

saucers

frying pan

stove

spoons

plates

iron

dish towel

cups

matches

brush

bowls

closet

7

The yard

wheelbarrow

beehive

snail

bricks

pigeon

shovel

ladybug

trash can

seeds

shed

watering can

worm

flowers

sprinkler

hoe

wasp

bee

trowel

bone

hedge

fork

lawn mower

path

leaves

tree

smoke

caterpillar

rake

nest

sticks

grass

baby buggy

vegetables

bonfire

garden hose

greenhouse

9

The workshop

screws

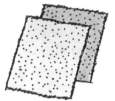
vise

sandpaper

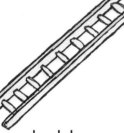
drill

ladder

saw

sawdust

calendar

toolbox

screwdriver

board

shavings

pocketknife

10

tacks

spider

bolts

nuts

cobweb

barrel

fly

ax

tape measure

hammer

file

paint can

plane

wood

nails

workbench

jars

11

The street

store

hole

café

ambulance

sidewalk

statue

chimney

roof

bulldozer

hotel

bus

man

police car

pipes

drill

school

playground

taxi

crosswalk

factory

truck

traffic lights

movie theater

van

steamroller

trailer

house

market

steps

motorcycle

bicycle

fire engine

policeman

car

woman

lamp post

apartments

13

The toyshop

train set

dice

recorder

robot

necklace

camera

beads

dolls

guitar

ring

dollhouse

harmonica

whistle

blocks

castle

submarine

trumpet

arrows

14

bow

parachute

boat

face paints

steamroller

masks

race car

rocking horse

bank

marbles

puppets

piano

spacemen

crane

playing cards

drums

soldiers

paints

rocket

15

swings

sandpit

picnic

kite

ice cream

dog

gate

path

frog

slide

The park

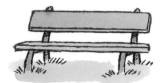
bench

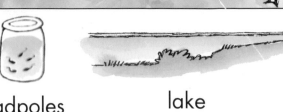
tadpoles

lake

roller blades

bush

16

 baby

 skateboard

 dirt

 stroller

 seesaw

 children

 tricycle

 birds

 fence

 ball

 boat

 string

 puddle

 ducklings

 jump-rope

 trees

 flower bed

swans

leash

 ducks

Animals

panda

wing

eagle

hippopotamus

bat

gorilla

paws

kangaroo

monkey

tail

wolf

iceberg

penguin

crocodile

bear

feathers

pelican

ostrich

dolphin

giraffe

lion

cubs

deer

camel

seal

polar bear

tortoise

elephant

trunk

rhinoceros

bison

horns

beaver

goat

zebra

snake

shark

whale

tiger

leopard

Travel

train track

engine

buffers

railway cars

engineer

freight train

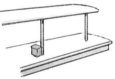
platform

conductor

suitcase

ticket machine

The railway station

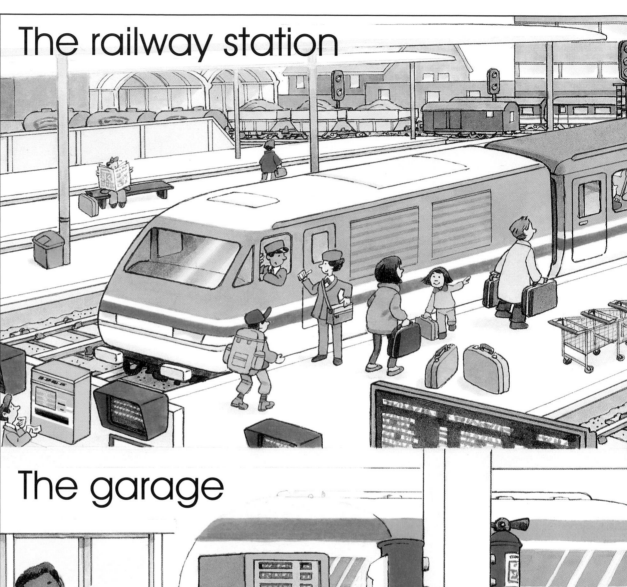

The garage

signals

backpack

headlights

engine

wheel

battery

plane

helicopter

runway

control tower

The airport

cabin crew

pilot

car wash

trunk

gas

tow truck

car wash

gas pump

tanker

wrench

tire

hood

oil

The country

windmill

hot-air balloon

butterfly

lizard

stones

fox

stream

signpost

porcupine

lock

mountain

squirrel

forest

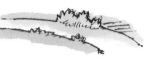

badger

river

road

tents

canal

logs

town

moth

bridge

barge

waterfall

owl

tunnel

fox cubs

mole

fisherman

rocks

toad

train

camper

hill

23

The farm

haystack

sheepdog

lambs

pond

chicks

hayloft

pigsty

bull

hen house

tractor

rooster

geese

tanker

barn

mud

cart

24

farmer

field

hens

calf

fence

saddle

cowshed

cow

plow

orchard

stable

piglets

donkey

turkeys

scarecrow

hay

sheep

straw bales

horse

pigs

farmhouse

The seaside

sailboat

sea

oar

lighthouse

shovel

bucket

starfish

sandcastle

umbrella

flag

sailor

shell

crab

seagull

island

motor-boat

water-skier

26

waves

sunhat

cliff

ship

kayak

rope

pebbles

seaweed

net

paddle

fishing boat

flippers

sunscreen

fish

swimsuit

oil tanker

beach

rowboat

beach chair

At school

scissors

$2 + 2 = 4$
$2 + 3 = 5$
sums

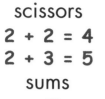

eraser

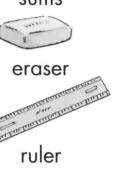

ruler

photographs

felt-tip pens

clay

paints

boy

pencil

board

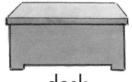

desk

books

pen

glue

chalk

drawing

wastepaper basket

teacher

box

map

brush

ceiling

wall

floor

a b c d e f
g h i j k l m
n o p q r s
t u v w x y z

notebook

a b c d e f
g h i j k l m
n o p q r s
t u v w x y z

alphabet

badge

aquarium

2 + 2 = 4
2 + 3 = 5

paper

blind

door handle

plant

globe

girl

crayons

lamp

easel

29

The hospital

nurse

cotton balls

medicine

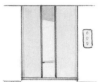
elevator

bathrobe

crutches

pills

tray

watch

apple

curtain

cast

bandage

wheelchair

jigsaw
puzzle

doctor

syringe

thermometer

The doctor

slippers

computer

adhesive bandage

banana

grapes

basket

toys

pear

cards

diaper

walking stick

pillow   nightgown   pajamas   orange   tissues   comic   waiting room

The party

presents

balloon

chocolate

glasses

candy

window

fireworks

ribbon

cake

straw

candle

paper chains

toys

32

tangerine

salami

teddy bear

sausage

chips

costumes

cherry

fruit juice

raspberry

strawberry

lightbulb

sandwich

butter

cookie

cheese

bread

tablecloth

33

The store

grapefruit

carrot

cauliflower

leek

mushroom

cucumber

lemon

celery

apricot

melon

grocery sack

CHEESE

FRUIT AND VEGETABLES

onion

cabbage

peach

lettuce

peas

tomato

eggs

plum

flour

scales

jars

meat

pineapple

yogurt

basket

bottles

purse

coin purse

money

cans

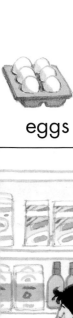

cart

potatoes

spinach

beans

checkout

pumpkin

35

Food

breakfast

lunch or dinner

coffee

boiled egg

fried egg

toast

jam

cream

milk

cereal

hot chocolate

sugar

tea

honey

salt

pepper

teapot

pancakes

rolls

supper or dinner

ham

soup

omelette

chopsticks

salad

hamburger

chicken

rice

ketchup

spaghetti

mashed potatoes

pizza

french fries

dessert

37

Me

head

hair

face

eyebrow

eye

nose

cheek

mouth

lips

arm

elbow

tummy

teeth

tongue

chin

ears

neck

shoulders

toes

foot

leg

knee

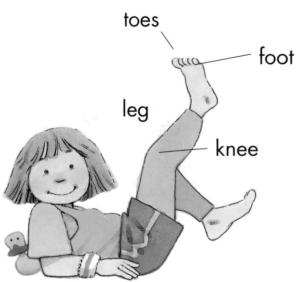

chest

back

bottom

hand

thumb

fingers

My clothes

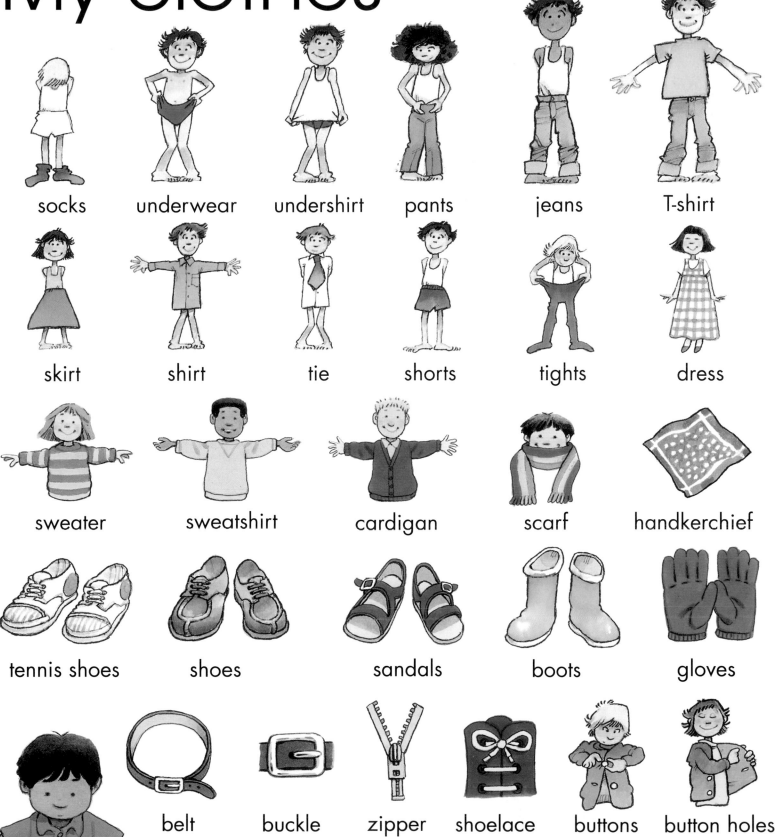

socks underwear undershirt pants jeans T-shirt

skirt shirt tie shorts tights dress

sweater sweatshirt cardigan scarf handkerchief

tennis shoes shoes sandals boots gloves

belt buckle zipper shoelace buttons button holes

pockets

coat

jacket

cap

hat

People

actor actress

chef

dancers

singers

astronaut

butcher

policeman

policewoman

carpenter

firefighter

artist

judge

mechanics

barber

truck driver

bus driver

waiter   waitress

mail carrier

dentist

diver

painter

baker

Families

son
brother

daughter
sister

mother
wife

father
husband

aunt   uncle

pet

cousin

grandfather

grandmother

41

Doing things

laugh

smile

cry

think

listen

catch

throw

break

paint

write

chop

cut

eat

talk

dig

carry

drink

make

jump

dance

wash

knit

crawl

play

watch

climb

fight

sleep

take

sew

skip

wait

cook

hide

read

buy

push

sweep

sing

pick

blow

pull

fall

walk

run

sit

43

Opposite words

good

bad

far

near

top

bottom

cold

hot

wet

dry

dirty

clean

over

under

fat

thin

open

closed

small

big

few

many

first

last

left

out

in

easy

difficult

empty

full

soft

hard

front

high

slow

fast

back

low

long

short

dead

alive

dark

light

old

upstairs

right

new

downstairs

45

Days

Sunday
Monday
Tuesday
Wednesday
Thursday
Friday
Saturday

calendar

morning

evening

sun

night

space

moon

star

planet

spaceship

telescope

46

Special days

birthday

present

candle

birthday card

birthday cake

vacation

wedding day

guests

bridesmaid

bride

bridegroom

camera

photographer

Christmas day

reindeer

sleigh

Santa Claus

Christmas tree

Weather

umbrella

rain

lightning

fog

sun

clouds

sky

snow

dew

wind

mist

frost

rainbow

Seasons

spring

summer

fall

winter

Pets

hamster

guinea pig

vet

kennel

dog

puppy

food

parakeet

parrot

beak

rabbit

canary

cage

cat

basket

mouse

kitten

milk

goldfish

Sports and exercise

basketball

rowing

sail

snowboarding

sailing

windsurfing

racket

tennis

football

gym

cricket

karate

bat

ball

dance

baseball

fishing rod

fishing

bait

rugby

diving

swimming pool

race

swimming

archery

target

hang-gliding

judo

jogging

cycling

helmet

climbing

soccer

horse

pony

locker

changing room

riding

badminton

table tennis

ice skates

ice-skating

ski pole

chairlift

ski

skiing

sumo wrestling

Colors

orange

green

black

gray

red

brown

white

blue

pink

purple

yellow

Shapes

rectangle

circle

diamond

cone

star

cube

oval

triangle

square

crescent

Numbers

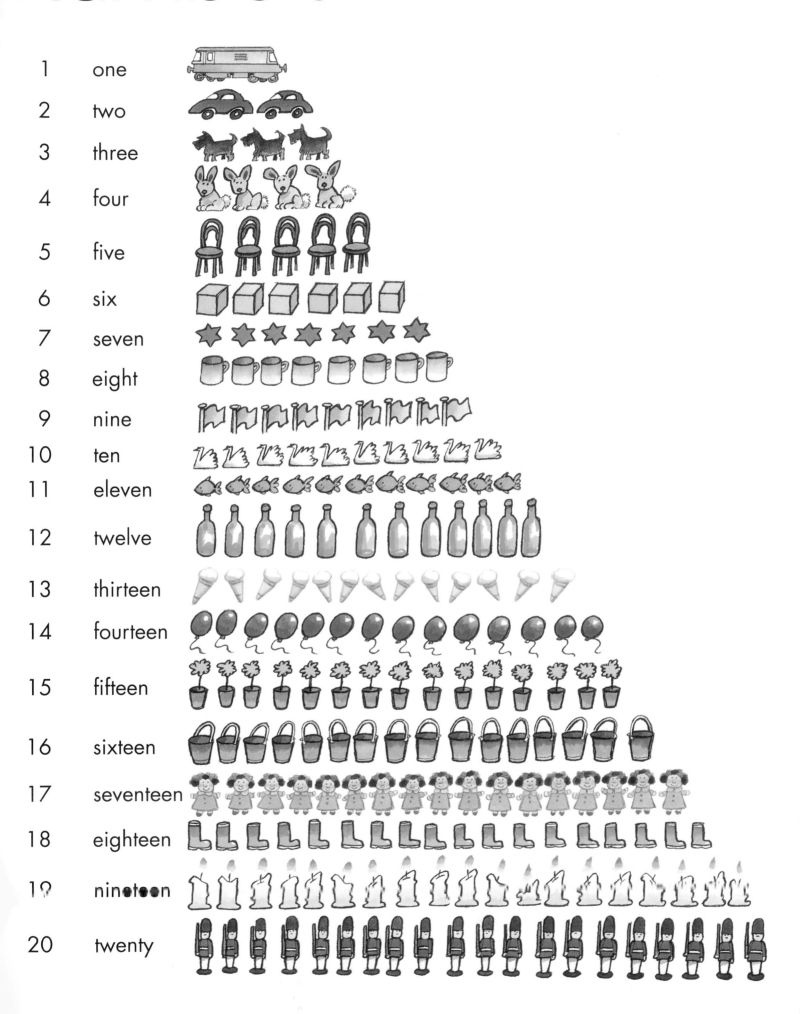

1	one
2	two
3	three
4	four
5	five
6	six
7	seven
8	eight
9	nine
10	ten
11	eleven
12	twelve
13	thirteen
14	fourteen
15	fifteen
16	sixteen
17	seventeen
18	eighteen
19	nineteen
20	twenty

The amusement park

Ferris wheel

merry-go-round

cotton candy

amusement ride

popcorn

slide

mat

bumper cars

ring toss

roller coaster

The circus

unicyclist

acrobats

juggler

trapeze

rope ladder

tightrope walker

pole

tightrope

safety net

rabbit

ringmaster

hoop

dog

top hat

bow tie

band

bareback rider

clown

Words in order

This is a list of all the words in the pictures, in alphabetical order. After each word is a page number. On that page, you will find the word and picture together.

a

acrobats, 55
actor, 40
actress, 40
adhesive bandage, 31
airport, 21
alive, 45
alphabet, 29
ambulance, 12
amusement park, 54
amusement ride, 54
animals, 18
apartments, 13
apple, 30
apricot, 34
apron, 6
aquarium, 29
archery, 51
arm, 38
arrows, 14
artist, 40
astronaut, 40
aunt, 41
ax, 11

b

baby, 17
baby buggy, 9
back (of body), 38
back (not front), 45
backpack, 20
bad, 44
badge, 29
badger, 22
badminton, 51

bait, 50
baker, 41
ball, 17, 50
balloon, 32
banana, 31
band, 55
bandage, 30
bank, 15
barber, 41
bareback rider, 55
barge, 23
barn, 24
barrel, 11
baseball, 50
basket, 31, 35, 49
basketball, 50
bat (animal), 18
bat (for sport), 50
bathtub, 4
bathrobe, 30
bathroom, 4
battery, 20
beach, 27
beach chair, 27
beads, 14
beak, 49
beans, 35
bear, 18
beaver, 19
bed, 4
bedroom, 5
bee, 9
beehive, 8
belt, 39
bench, 16
bicycle, 13
big, 44
birds, 17
birthday, 47
birthday cake, 47
birthday card, 47
bison, 19
black, 52
blind (for a window), 29
blocks, 14

blow, 43
blue, 52
board, 10, 28
boat, 15, 17
boiled egg, 36
bolts, 11
bone, 9
bonfire, 9
books, 28
boots, 39
bottles, 35
bottom (of body), 38
bottom (not top), 44
bow, 15
bowls, 7
bow tie, 55
box, 29
boy, 28
bread, 33
break, 42
breakfast, 36
bricks, 8
bride, 47
bridegroom, 47
bridesmaid, 47
bridge, 23
broom, 7
brother, 41
brown, 52
brush, 5, 7, 29
bucket, 26
buckle, 39
buffers, 20
bull, 24
bulldozer, 12
bumper cars, 54
bus, 12
bus driver, 41
bush, 16
butcher, 40
butter, 33
butterfly, 22
button holes, 39
buttons, 39
buy, 43